This is Portland

the city you've heard you should like

Alexander Barrett

Microcosm Publishing
Portland, OR

First printing of 6,000 copies, May 1, 2013
Second printing of 5,000 copies, January 15, 2014
Third printing of 7,000 copies, October 15, 2014
Fourth printing of 7,000 copies, March 15, 2016
Fifth printing of 7,000 copies, April 15, 2017

Microcosm Publishing, 2752 N Williams Ave., Portland, OR 97227
MicrocosmPublishing.com
Carefully printed on post-consumer paper in the United States
Distributed by PGW and Turnaround UK
ISBN 978-1-62106-024-6

Library of Congress Cataloging-in-Publication Data

Names: Barrett, Alexander, 1983- author.
Title: This is Portland : the city you've heard you should like / Alexander
   Barrett.
Description: Portland, OR : Microcosm Publishing, 2017.
Identifiers: LCCN 2016050788 | ISBN 9781621060246 (pbk.)
Subjects: LCSH: Portland (Or.)--Description and travel. | Portland
   (Or.)--Social life and customs.
Classification: LCC F884.P84 B37 2017 | DDC 979.5/49--dc23
LC record available at https://lccn.loc.gov/2016050788

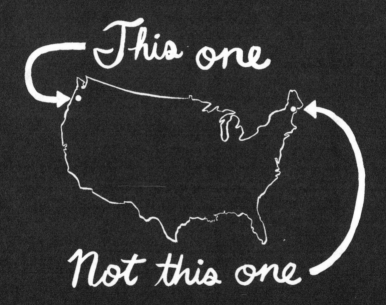

I have lived in Portland, Oregon for one year and one month. Before I moved here, everyone told me it was the best city ever. When I asked them why, they couldn't be specific. I heard a lot of: "It just is."

This is my attempt to be specific.

Not all of the things in this book are exclusive to Portland, but together, they'll give you an idea of how Portland makes me feel. This feeling will hopefully show you exactly why Portland, Oregon, is, hands down, the best city ever.

the Rain

When you start talking about visiting or moving to Portland, people are going to warn you about the rain. Apparently, the consensus between everyone I know is that they'd like to live in Portland, but they just can't deal with the oppressive, ever-present rain.

Here is Portland's greatest secret: It doesn't rain that much. It's a little gloomy for most of the winter, but it only occasionally gets really serious about raining. It drizzles, sure, but anyone can manage a drizzle.

I don't want to seem paranoid, but there is absolutely a conspiracy at work here. Portlanders over-hype the rain in order to keep outsiders from moving in. When tourists visit in summer and think Portland is a paradise on earth and the answer to all of their problems, the locals say, "Sure, but this only lasts for four months. The rest of our life here is a wet, cloudy, living hell. Save yourself! Get out while you still can!" And then the tourists back away slowly and leave the city forever, allowing the locals to stretch their legs, and making the lines at Pine State Biscuits much shorter.

It might not be ethical, but it works.

Okay, I started writing this in January. It is now March. It rains plenty here. It rains about 37.5 inches a year. I'm not part of this conspiracy. I am actually annoyed. It is oppressive. It is ever-present. I'm told it won't stop until the Fourth of July. Save yourself! Get out while you still can!

Reading this over, I'm worrying that I may be focusing too much on the weather right off the bat. Weather shouldn't make a city. But in Portland's case, it really does. Everything about Portland changes with the seasons. And by seasons, I'm talking about Rain and Summer. During the rain, Portland is dreary, but it's still a great city. During the summer, it borders on heaven.

More on that later.

One more observation about the rain: Portland is full of cool people. Raincoats are not cool. How do cool people stay cool in the rain? They get really wet, that's how.

Nickname City

Portland hates calling itself "Portland." It has a lot of nicknames and it's pretty hard to keep track of them. Here's a convenient list, so you'll have them all in one place.

1. City of Roses

There are two possible reasons for Portland's official nickname.

a. In 1871, Leo Samuel moved to Portland. He always kept perfectly groomed rose bushes on his front lawn. A pair of clippers sat next to the bushes so passersby could snip off a flower and take it with them, perhaps for use as a boutonniere. In 1906, Samuel founded the Oregon Life Insurance Company.

b. During an 1888 Episcopal Church convention, someone said something about

Portland being "the City of Roses." The name didn't really go anywhere for the next seventeen years. Then, Mayor Harry Lane spoke before the 1905 Lewis and Clark Centennial Exposition and declared that the city needed a festival of roses. Two years later, the festival of roses began. It and the nickname have been going strong ever since.

2. Bridgetown

Here's the thing about Portland: It has a lot of bridges.

3. Rip City

On February 18th, 1971, the Portland Trail Blazers, then in their first season, were playing against the Los Angeles Lakers. The Lakers were ahead, it seemed all hope was lost. Then, guard Jim Barnett sank a shot from way downtown. Blazers announcer Bill Schonely, overcome with excitement, shouted: "Rip city! Alright!" It had nothing to do with anything. It was perfect.

4. P-Town

Some people call Portland P-town. I've never met these people, but I'm sure they lead rich, colorful lives.

5. Stumptown

In the mid-to-late 1840's, Portland's population was growing fast. People were settling farther and farther away from the city and trees had to be cut down to make way for new roads. While there were plenty of workers to do the cutting, there was no one to remove the stumps. So, the stumps remained while the city waited for more manpower.

Some people walked on the stumps to avoid the mud. Some people painted the stumps white to make sure the city knew they were still there. When businessman John C. Ainsworth came to town in the early 1850's, he quipped that there were "more stumps than trees." No one was amused, but they'd figured it would be a good nickname.

6. Razorblade City

Portland has a pretty high depression and suicide rate. It gets dark in the winter. The Lifesavas, a local hip-hop group, coined the nickname on their 2007 album, *Gutterfly*. Despite their name, the suicide rate has not gone down since The Lifesavas got together.

7. PDX

PDX is the airport code for the Portland International Airport. There's an "x" in it, so people think it sounds cool.

8. Little Beirut

Whenever President George Herbert Walker Bush came to town he was always greeted by throngs of protestors. His staffers labeled the city "Little Beirut."

They were all assholes.

Bands

If you live in Portland and you aren't in a band, people will look at you funny at concerts. They'll ask: "So, when are you going up?" And you'll say: "Oh, no, I just came to hear some music."

Then they'll give you the stink eye and back away slowly.

Food Carts

As I'm writing this, there are about 700 registered food carts in Multnomah County. Not all of them are in city limits. But believe me, a whole lot of them are. As soon as this book is released, that number will go up. Actually, that number will probably go up tomorrow, but let's just stick with "about 700." That sounds impressive enough, right?

More and more, when you walk down the street, you'll pass what was, until recently, an empty lot but now is filled with tiny trailers or little shacks, each serving a different kind of food. If Portland is one giant Shopping Mall, these are the food courts.

You'll find the most impressive collection downtown at SW 9th and Alder. A full city block of carts. All you have to do is walk around and take your pick. It sounds a lot easier than it is.

Cart indecision can be a real problem. If you are one of the lucky ones who can easily make a choice, look around you while you wait for your food. You'll see tourists bewildered by options. You'll see locals taking fake phone calls, walking up and down the block, trying to make it seem like they know what they're doing. You'll see the moment that a group of co-workers realizes that none of them want to go to the same place. Each one will end up walking back to the office alone. And you'll see old pros who've narrowed it down to their two favorite places. Their eyes dart back and forth as they weigh the pros and cons because at this moment, they're facing the most important decision in their lives.

People in other cities are used to seeing hot dog carts, fruit carts, maybe a Halal cart here and there. But in Portland, you get everything. One of my favorite pizzas in the city comes from a cart that's next to my favorite poutine which is next to my favorite milkshake. It's a Cinnamon Toast Crunch milkshake. Jealous?

So why are there this many? The same reason restaurants are so jealous of them: You don't have to pay rent, you don't need to hire a staff, and to be successful, you only really have to know how to make one thing really well. Portland appreciates a specialty. The people don't just want to hear about where they should eat, they want to know what that place does better than anyone else.

Take Nong's on SW Alder. They make chicken on rice with a drinking broth. That's the menu. They can't offer you anything else. There's a line every day.

You hear about a place that makes a great thing, you go, you enjoy it on a bench and look at the cart across the way. Next time, you gotta try that place. The cycle continues.

the Portland Driver

The Portland Driver hates the right of way.

He avoids it at all costs.

If he sees a cyclist twenty feet from a stop sign, he will jam on the brakes and let them pass.

If he sees someone leaving a house, he will slow down just to see if that person would like to cross the street.

If four Portland Drivers come to a four way stop, they will all put their cars in park, walk to the middle of the intersection, and explain to each other that they didn't really feel like driving that day anyway.

The Portland Driver is a very nice person.

Way too nice.

What the sign says:

What the Portland Driver
thinks it says:

Strip Clubs

Portland is home to more strip clubs per capita than any other U.S. city. This is true. Portland has more strip clubs per capita than Las Vegas.

At first, it doesn't make sense. "All I can see here are coffee shops and record stores." Then after a week, they start revealing themselves to you. And they don't stop. There are well over 50 strip clubs in the greater metropolitan area. It is at once awe-inspiring and just a touch shady. It really is mostly awe-inspiring, though.

So, why? Why does the most pleasant, quiet city in the United States have more professional naked ladies than anywhere else? There are two reasons. First, the Oregon state constitution protects first amendment rights like crazy. In 1987, the Oregon Supreme Court found that full nudity and lap dances are protected speech in Henry v. Oregon Constitution.

Second, Portland used to be a sketchy place. It was stabbing sketchy. It was human trafficking sketchy. Back around the time of the gold rush, Portland was basically lawless. It was exactly the kind of place that could support a vibrant sex industry. Over the years, as the human trafficking reduced and the stabbing rate went down considerably, the strip clubs remained.

They're just a part of the culture now. In many areas, it's easier to get to a strip club than it is to get to the supermarket. And that doesn't bother anybody. I'm sure it bothered somebody at some point. The Henry from "Henry v. Oregon Constitution," I bet he was bothered. But people like Henry have been shouted down for years. By now, they've either learned to accept it or moved away.

There's something funny about knowing that no matter where you are, you could be at a strip club in ten minutes. Many times, I've asked my coworkers: "What are you up to tonight?" And they say: "I don't know. Nothing. I'm pretty tired and I think I'm getting sick." A half an hour later, I'm getting drunk texts from the rack at Sassy's.

The next day, when I ask how they ended up there, they just shrug.

It's just what you do.

Keep Portland Weird

Portland's number one bumper sticker is :
"KEEP PORTLAND WEIRD"

After a year of living in Portland, I'm still not sure to what weirdness it is referring. There has never been a moment where I've felt the need to just stand up and say: "This city is really weird." I'd call it kooky at best. And even then, only on rare occasions. Maybe during the annual naked bike ride. But all those people know exactly how kooky they're being. It's doesn't count.

I saw one pretty weird homeless guy one time. He had a pretty weird hat. But the city is too nice to call that man weird. I've seen plenty of aging hippies, but I'm from Vermont. Our aging hippies put Portland's aging hippies to shame. Our hippies' VW Vans are a lot smellier, too.

I've been to plenty of Portland's art openings and punk shows. All are pretty much what you'd expect: pretty fun and pretty cool.

So what the hell is this bumper sticker talking about?

I have an idea for a replacement:

KEEP PORTLAND
PORTLAND!

SE v. NE

At this point in the book, you're probably ready to move to Portland. Congratulations, I think this is a great decision. Now you're probably wondering where in the city I think you should move. That's easy. I'm an east side guy.

Portland is split right down the middle by the Willamette River. On the West Side, you'll find the downtown area. It's the part of the city that looks like a city. The Northwest is more residential. Things close early there. The Southwest has Portland State University. There's a hospital down there too. I'll be honest with you, I went down there once for a party and I've never been back. That party got real weird.

On the east side, it doesn't even feel like you're living in a city. It feels like a sleepy, small town that decided to get cool. Most of it is residential, with pockets of shops, restaurants, parks, bars, movie theaters, and coffee, coffee, a lot of coffee.

If you work on the west side, it's more of a hike, but I like riding my bike over the river every morning. And if you're meeting friends for a night on the town, you just ride over Burnside bridge and see a tiny, little metropolis unfolding before you. From half a mile away, you can see the whole city, all lit up.

It's like the beginning of *Bladerunner*. Except way more adorable.

Now you're probably saying: "Sounds great. East side. You've sold me. So should I live in Northeast or Southeast?" That's where things start to get tricky.

Both have amazing shops, restaurants, parks, bars, movie theaters, and coffee, coffee, a lot of coffee. They are equally fantastic places to be. I'm just south of the border, so I can't choose. Please don't make me choose. Most people who live on the east side, however, have a very strong opinion on the matter. And I think I know the reason why.

If you ask someone who lives in the Northeast, they'll say the Northeast is better. If you ask someone who lives in the Southeast, they'll say the Southeast is better. And it's simply because they want to drink close to their house.

If you live in the Northeast and a friend is having a get together in the Southeast, you either have to bike or drive. Let's face it, if you're going to the get together, you're gonna drink. And when you get to that four beer mark, nobody wants to deal with a bus.

If you're asking a friend where to move, their goal is to get you to move close to them so there's less a chance of you having a party elsewhere.

My advice: Throw a dart at a map. You'll be happy either way.

Tattoos

I'd like to preface this by saying that even after a year and a month in Portland, I still do not have a tattoo. I'll try my best not to sound like an unhip suburban mom.

In Portland, there are twelve tattoo parlors for every 100,000 people. That's a lot of tattoo parlors. How can that many businesses sustain themselves in one, medium-sized city? You'll know why as soon as you walk down any street.

Tattoos are everywhere. And they're on every single kind of person.

There's a janitor at the school down the street with the cover of the *Dungeon Master's Guide* on his forearm.

Your company's IT guy has an ice cream sundae on his chest.

One night, you'll be out to a fancy meal and your server will have the *Thrasher Magazine* logo tattooed across his or her neck.

I once bought a book at a yard sale from a mom with a tattoo of a hippie mushroom on her face. Surprisingly, her children seemed well balanced. (Okay, I got a little bit suburban mom just then. Sorry.)

Tattoos are another holdover from Portland's wild west history. Sure, the city has gotten a whole lot more pleasant, but its people want to remind you that Portland is and always will be a city of badasses.

Tater Tots

In Portland, every bar that serves liquor is required by law to serve at least three hot food items and two cold food items. This is probably why the "gastropub" has become such an institution. These are bars with great beer, great food, and great atmosphere.

But what if you don't care about great food? What if you just want to sell watery beer and booze? What if you just want to open a shithole?

Tots.

Tater Tots are cheap and easy. All you need to do is open a bag and dump them into a Fry-o-lator. You can even leave them in too long if you want. Past golden brown and on their way to black is a Portland standard. It doesn't matter, I really won't mind because I'm definitely drunk and anything you put in front of me is going to be manna from heaven.

"Are these spicy Tots or regular, because I ordered regular," I might ask as you place a basket in front of me. "Oh, these are spicy let me just get you a…" you won't finish your sentence. I don't care. The basket will be snatched from your hands and my mouth will be full of delicious fried potato cylinders within seconds. Your tip will be generous.

I know that Tater Tots are ubiquitous. They are American. Portland doesn't own them. But for me, no night out in Portland is complete without a basket. No matter where I go, they'll always remind me of great times, great people, and riding the bus home, completely satisfied and sometimes asleep.

Oh, and for all you new bar owners: while you've got that Fry-o-lator going, why not throw in a bag of fries and a few corndogs? There's your three hot menu items.

Oh, right, you need two cold items. How about a bag of chips and a plate of iceberg lettuce coated with the cheapest ranch dressing you can possibly find?

Perfect.

The Most Optimistic Place in the World

Portland is the most optimistic place I've ever been. It's not the people who live there. It's not the strong sensation of civic pride.

It's the overwhelming amount of outdoor seating.

Restaurants and Bars with benches, tables and chairs set up outside all year long. The benches are weather beaten. The tables spend most of the year caked in dirt.

if you move to Portland in the winter, you could visit bars over and over, you could have a favorite bar and not even know they have a one acre backyard with 20 Cornhole games set up. And yes, they do hold Cornhole tournaments. Every summer is like a never-ending Cornhole tournament.

Many new restaurants have entire front walls that open like garage doors. For eight months out of the year you think: "Wow, that is a weird looking wall, why would anybody choose to build a wall like that?" Then, the first week of July you could be sitting in a bar feeling like you're enjoying a margarita by the pool.

It might seem silly to an outsider, but this seating is about more than just summer fun. In the dead of winter, when you've been wet for months on end, when your body has just given up on melatonin, and when you're ready to rent the moving van tomorrow, you'll head into a bar to drink away your sorrows, and you'll see this seating. Then, you're transported back to the good times. And you're reminded that these times will come again.

So you stay strong. When the summer comes, you'll spend every meal and every drink outside. And when you go inside to hit the restroom, you'll roll your eyes at all the tourists sitting inside.

And you'll yell at them:

"What are you, a goth? GO OUTSIDE!"

the Snow

The winter isn't all rain. For a few hours of those eight months, it snows, too. But you'd better enjoy it while you can.

Late one night in January, I was walking home from a friend's house. It began to snow. I was excited. It was the first time in a long time that it was snowing where I lived.

Sure, I see snow when I go back to New England for the holidays, but this was different. This was my snow and I was going to have a magical walk home.

Halfway through my one mile walk, the snow stopped and the little that had accumulated on the ground had already melted. I was completely dry when I entered my apartment.

And yes, the next morning, every public school called a snow day.

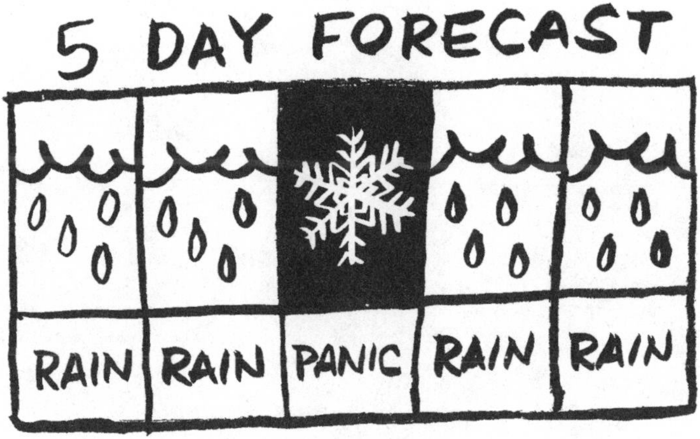
5 DAY FORECAST
RAIN
RAIN
PANIC
RAIN
RAIN

Bikes

Portland has a shitload of bikes.

Beer

Portland has a shitload of beer.

Beards

Portland has a shitload of beards.

the Sun

When the sun comes out in Portland, the city changes.

All spring, there are hints of how good it's going to be. It's a Saturday morning, you walk outdoors and there are no clouds. Suddenly, you see people emerging from their homes, looking at the sky, confused. Everyone just stands there, soaking up the vitamin D. A few minutes later, they snap out of their stupor. They say: "Oh. Outside! I get it! This is how life used to be!" Sunglasses are uncovered, bikes are taken out of storage, and men remember what women are. People point their cameras toward the sky, take a picture off pure blue and immediately post it online. The caption will be a series of capitalized vowels followed by a field of exclamation points. But this is just a tease, because it will rain again.

The city has to wait for the Fourth of July. After that, there won't be rain for four months. That four months is what Portland is all about.

This city wears its Winter like a badge of honor. It is 600,000 who have all agreed to live through a damp, eight month nightmare because when it finally comes to an end, they will know perfection: the Portland Summer.

The Portland Summer is many things, but mostly, it's:

Barbeques,

Barbeques,

Barbeques,

Barbeques,

and

Barbeques.

Barbecues every night of the week and three times a day on weekends. It is the ultimate summer, because you've earned it.

You stuck out that winter and you were wet for eight months. This is yours by right and you will stand tall with a hamburger in one hand and a cheap beer in the other.

Fancy Junk food

"Sometimes foods." My mom had been warning me about them since I was old enough to pull a chair over to the refrigerator, open the freezer, and get my hands on those sweet popsicles. They're the foods you only have once in a while, because if you had them all the time, you'd be fat.

Portland has turned "sometimes foods" into high art.

It's turned "sometimes" into "all the time."

Wherever you go, you'll find foods that you definitely shouldn't be eating, but hey, you're finally standing in front of this place that you've heard so much about and they have that maple bacon whatever that everyone's been telling you to try. So you do.

And you justify it because hey, it's artisanal.

I really like running. I'd go as far as saying that I am a runner. In Portland, it rains a lot. I'm not crazy about running in the rain. I'm kind of a baby. I do not, however, mind eating fancy junk food in the rain. That suits me just fine.

This is a problem.

One day, I was at Lovely's Fifty Fifty, eating a transcendental salted caramel ice cream cone. One of my friends said they perfered the salted caramel at Salt and Straw. What were we going to do, not go to Salt and Straw and get another ice cream?

Needless to say, I have gained weight in Portland and it has been delicious.

Consider yourself warned.

The Most Portland Thing I Have Ever Seen.

I have witnessed two events that tie for the title of "the most Portland thing I have ever seen." Feel free to judge for yourself.

1. As I rode my bike west on Southeast Ankeny Street, I approached what I thought was another bike and prepared to pass. When I got closer, I saw that the rider was sitting three feet above me, but this wasn't a "tall bike." As I passed, I finally knew what I was looking at: a giant unicycle. This unicycle's rider was wearing khakis, a polo shirt, and had a padded messenger bag on his back. It wasn't just a giant unicycle. It was a giant commuter unicycle.

There was even a fender connected to the back seat. This guy planned to ride through the rain all winter.

So why is this a perfect symbol for Portland? It's alternative, business casual, stubbornly ecofriendly, it doesn't care how stupid it looks, and it involves the suffix "cycle." He should be the Grand Marshal of the Rose Parade. The city's flag should just be his picture. This guy should get a key to the city and his likeness should be engraved on the key's side.

2. It was spring. Somehow, the sun was out which meant that everyone was on the street. I was walking west over the Burnside Bridge to meet some friends. Up ahead, a tricycle for hire with a two-passenger back seat, or "Pedicab," was approaching slowly.

The Pedicab driver was just starting to climb the bridge's incline, and was having a pretty difficult time. I looked in the backseat. In it were two morbidly obese Goth women. They were both smoking. The driver would pedal once, recover for a second, and then pedal again. I really felt for him, but what could I do?

Just then, an elderly couple began to walk across the bridge. They looked like they were enjoying a lovely day. It was easy to see that they were runners. They had the shoes, they had the hats, and they were both in great shape. As soon as the elderly man saw the Pedicab driver struggling, he ran out into the street, greeted the two Goth women, and started pushing the Pedicab up the hill. I had to stop myself from cheering.

So why is this a perfect symbol for Portland? It involves two alternative ladies, running culture, ecofriendliness, a man going beyond the call of politeness, and the suffix "cycle." I felt like taking the whole group to Voodoo Donuts, then over to Stumptown, where we'd sit and laugh and feel good about our city.

Cars

There was a two month period where I forgot about my car. That's how good the busses are in this city and that's how easy it is to bike around. I owned a car and I just forgot about it for two months.

When I finally realized I still owned a car it was like being in one of those dreams where you're in college. It's finals week and you've just remembered you have a class that you'd forgotten about all semester and the final is right now and if you don't get an A they're going to kick you out of school.

I hadn't laid eyes on my car. Was it parked around the corner? I had no idea. Would there be tickets? How much trouble was I in?

When I got home and found my car, I realized that I was wrong to worry. I was in Portland.

In what other city could you leave a car parked on the street for two months and still own a car? How was it not stolen? How was it not impounded? How did all of those windows remain unsmashed? How did roving bands of teenagers not even think to key it? How did I not get a single ticket?

I got in my car, started it up and moved it ten feet.

Then, I left it there for three weeks.

the '99 Subaru Legacy

a.k.a.

the Portland Escalade

Hawthorne v. Belmont

Hawthorne Boulevard is by far the hippest street in the Southeast. It's the worst. The ten block strip that is the "Hawthorne District" is home of every bad Portland stereotype. Lazy twenty-somethings, the craziest homeless people, the dirtiest hippies, the loudest petitioners, buskers every 10 feet, fashionable young parents with the widest strollers available in the United States, they're all there in full force.

Generally, I'm a nice guy, but Hawthorne Boulevard turns me into a raging neo-conservative. "GET A JOB!" I shout in my head to almost everyone who walks by, completely forgetting that I too have no job. "HEY, TRY SOME BIRTH CONTROL!" I shout in my head to the young parents, completely forgetting that I'm a conservative in this scenario and would be in favor of them having children—in wedlock, obviously.

If you come for a visit, there's a good chance someone will tell you to spend an afternoon walking around Hawthorne. If they do, thank them for their advice and ignore it. Instead, go to Belmont. Belmont Street is home to every good Portland stereotype. It's green, it has great restaurants, it has cool, young parents with reasonably sized strollers, and it's peaceful.

Also, I live there. And I can tell you there's nothing like waking up early on a Saturday morning, walking over to Pine State Biscuits, getting a huge breakfast, spending all day in the sun, making your way over to Horse Brass Pub in the evening, and drinking just enough so you'll need to get Pine State again the next morning. That's a life I am proud to lead.

The very best part of Belmont, though, is that it's only six blocks from Hawthorne. So, if a friend suggests you spend the afternoon hanging out with them on Hawthorne, you can make a break for it and go somewhere nice.

Chickens

If you have a backyard and you don't keep chickens, many will suspect you of being a republican.

$3 Movies

In Portland, it's easier to pay $3 for a movie than it is to pay $10. This is especially true in the southeast. There are two second run theaters within three blocks of my apartment. Within a mile, there are another two. If I want to see a new movie, I have to get in the car and drive at least three miles to a mall or somewhere very close to a mall. It's not nice there. And the worst part is, once I get there, I won't be able to find the two things that make Portland's second run theaters truly great: pizza and beer.

For less than the price of a first run movie ticket, popcorn, and a soda, you can get a second run movie ticket, a full meal of totally satisfactory pizza, and you can be drunk. What a beautiful idea. When you walk out of a late movie at the Laurelhurst Theater on SE 28th and Burnside, you're greeted with a jar sitting next to all the pizza the theater couldn't sell that night. There's a sign on the jar inviting you to pay whatever you want for a slice. The first time I saw this, I almost cried.

Whenever a magazine comes out with a "most livable cities in America" list, Portland is always on it. The articles talk about biking, dining, public transportation.

I read an article recently that said Portland's livability index is 100.3. I don't know what that means, but I guarantee you 100 whatevers of those 100.3 whatevers is eating a pizza and having a beer at the movies.

Full disclosure: I lied a little bit. Not all of these theaters have pizza and beer. There's one that doesn't: The Avalon. Instead, it has a full arcade where every game costs a nickel. The movies only cost $2.50, too.

What a nightmare.

Bad Burritos

Portland was never destined to be a good burrito town. One reason is, of course, that there are way too many white people here. I don't think they know any different. Portland doesn't really make burritos, it makes vaguely Mexican food bundles. A few of the bundles even taste okay, but they're just not burritos. I bought a "burrito" recently that had four full stalks of asparagus inside. Stop it, Portland. You're embarrassing yourself.

Maybe this doesn't seem like a big deal. Maybe they don't have good burritos where you live. I was once like you. If I had moved to Portland right after college, I would be perfectly happy. But I didn't. I made a three-year stop in Los Angeles where I learned that my quality of life increases with the quality of available burritos.

Someday, I'm going to have a craving for a chile relleno burrito so intense that I'll be forced to move away.

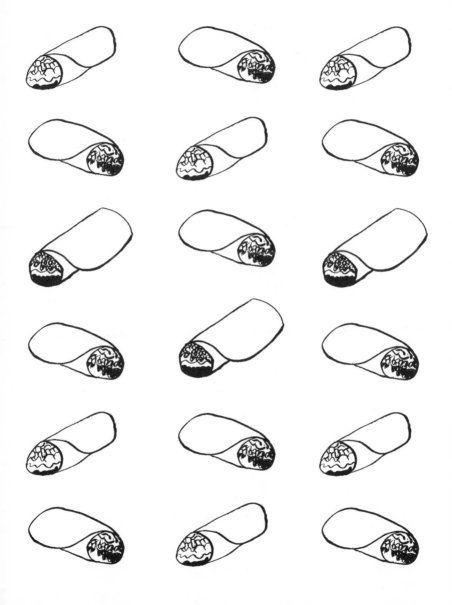

the Fish Hatchery

Listen, I know the hatchery isn't in Portland, but it's less than an hour drive and I want to talk about it. So, all the purists who were reading this expecting to only hear about things in the Portland metropolitan area, you just deal with it for two pages.

One day, I had nothing to do. I was getting antsy and just needed to get into my car and drive somewhere. I looked at a map and said: "Bonneville Dam. I've heard of that. That sounds like a guided tour I can get behind."

So I drove. Just before I got to the Dam, I saw a sign pointing towards a fish hatchery. I took no notice and continued. An hour later, I had finished a guided tour and discovered something about myself: I have a wide spectrum of interests, but unfortunately, guided tours of dams don't fall anywhere near it. I went back to Portland.

The next day, I went to work and told the tale of my non-adventure. Every person I talked to asked if I had gone to the fish hatchery. I told them no. Then they all exploded.

"WHAT ABOUT HERMAN!?" they shouted. There was a look is disappointment in their eyes.

A few weeks later, I went back to the hatchery and I understood why. Because that's when I met Herman, the 70 year old, 11 foot long, 500 pound White Sturgeon.

He lives there in his own little man-made pond, surrounded by smaller Sturgeon friends and children with their faces pressed against viewing windows. And to be honest, I was standing right alongside them.

Over the past twenty years, I've had a hard time dealing with the fact that I will never see a living dinosaur. Watching Herman pass back and forth across that pond was a pretty okay consolation prize.

After fifteen minutes of me gawking at Herman, the woman I brought was starting to get restless.* So, we got back in the car and headed to Hood River, Oregon, where we had a very nice day.

*Yes, I took a date to look at a big fish. Don't judge me.

People From Where You're From.

I'm from Vermont. Not originally, and I haven't lived there lately, but that's what I tell people at parties. As soon as I do, they run down a list of people they know from Vermont who live in Portland. And, crazily enough, there are always two at the party. So, I'm led across the room and introduced to my fellow Vermonters, and we take turns saying: "I miss Vermont, but Portland is great."

In my first three months here, I saw two people from my hometown on the bus. In December, I went to a holiday party where the girl who sat next to me in 11th grade chemistry told me she'd just moved into an apartment two blocks from mine. People from Vermont love Portland. And why shouldn't they? It's exactly the same.

They're both green, they're both close to adventure sports destinations, and they're both incredibly livable, sometimes too livable. It's very easy to stagnate in Vermont. People there tend to hang out and do whatever forever. Sometimes, people need to prove to themselves and/or their parents that they're doing something with their lives, but they don't really want their lives to change at all. So, they move to Portland.

But it's not just Vermont. No matter where you're coming from, this will happen to you. One of my friends moved up from San Diego, only to run into a good friend's cousin. Another moved from Ohio. When I asked him how many people from Ohio live in Portland, he said: "I think about 90% of the population."

It seems like a coincidence, but it isn't. People are coming to Portland and they're coming from all over. The city is getting bigger but at the same time, it's getting more familiar.

Portland and Seattle lead a pretty harmonious existence. They don't bicker. Their citizens visit each other regularly. They're happy being parts one and two of Pacific Northwest vacations.

But it seems that around the time of the Grunge movement, Seattle took a step forward. It became the "Big City," even though it's population isn't that much bigger than Portland's. And Portland was there screaming to the nation: HEY! WE HAVE COOL BANDS TOO!" But no one was listening.

Seattle took center stage and left Portland behind. That's when Portland said: "Okay, if that's the way it's going to be, we're going to fight back. We won't rest until we've taken the thing you hold most dear: coffee."

Cut to 20 years later: Portland has a shitload of coffee.

It seems like every few months, a new coffee place opens. And each is more intense than the last. The beans are somehow from a more pure source, the techniques have been handed down from generations in some remote land, the baristas are more serious about their craft than ever before. You'll hear this sentence a lot: "Oh that guy? He's a barista's barista."

And there's actually a coffee shop that's just called "Barista," where they not only sell different kinds of coffee, they sell different brands of those different kinds. You won't order decaf if you know what's good for you.

And so it shall remain. The city will be ever filled with coffee shops until the day the world recognizes Portland as the equal of Seattle.

The better of Seattle would be nice, too.

the Swifts

Vaux's Swift is a very small bird that likes to nest in chimney's all over the West Coast.

In the last week of September, thousands of them set up camp in the chimney of Chapman Elementary School in NW Portland.

Every night of that week, they return to the chimney after a day of hunting insects. But they don't return one at a time. They show up in a giant, swirling swarm. They circle the school, then form a funnel and disappear inside.

It's stunning.

This is an attraction. People pack picnic dinners and arrive early with their lawn chairs and blankets. They're not only there to see the swifts. They're there to celebrate the last event of summer. When this week is over, those lawn chairs won't see the light of day for a long, long time.

It's a perfect way to end on a high note. To sit back with some potato salad and reflect on all those trips to the river, all those barbecues, all those cornhole tournaments. It's a goodbye to summer.

And then, there are the hawks.

When the swifts are circling the chimney, the local hawks take notice. They like eating swifts and every night, they'll catch a few. The audience's reaction to this natural act says a lot about Portland:

They boo.

When you're in Portland, you never really have to deal with anything you hate. It's pleasant. It's bike paths and bakeries and community art centers and all the cheap beer you can handle. People love it here because they don't have to feel bad. So when they see a nice bird die, they say: "BOOOO, I came to watch that nice bird do a nice thing!"

This is what makes Portland a magical place to live. It's what makes you a softer, more sensitive person. Whether that's a good or bad thing, I'll leave up to you.

Oh, there are always a few people who cheer on the hawk. Portland is also about being a rebel.

References

Pine State Biscuits
They make biscuits. They're really good. Pine State has three locations. There's a big one on Alberta in the northeast, but I've never been to it because I lived 30 feet from the location on Belmont.

2204 NE Alberta St
Portland, OR 97211
Monday thru Wed 7a - 3p
Thursday thru Sunday 7a - 11p

Laurelhurst Theater
It's just a great second run theater. They even show one classic a week. I saw *Groundhog Day* there. Just go.

2735 East Burnside Street
Portland, OR 97214

The Avalon

The Avalon is in an arcade called Electric Castles Wunderland. From the outside, it looks like a clown porn theater.

3451 SE Belmont Street
Portland, OR 97214-4246
Sunday through Friday 12pm - 12am
Saturday 11am - 12am

Sassy's Bar & Grill

Sassy's is the default strip club for everyone I know. It has a really high, unfinished ceiling, which makes it feel like you're in a sexy, sexy barn.

927 SE Morrison St
Portland, OR 97214
Everyday 10:30am - 2am

Horse Brass Pub

Horse Brass is a British pub in the middle of Portland. The beer selection is so extensive that it's almost impossible to choose. Just get something you've never heard of, it'll be great.

4534 Southeast Belmont Street
Portland, OR 97215
Weekdays 11am - 2:30am
Weekends 9am - 2:30am

The Hawthorne Carts

This is where you'll find Pyro Pizza (an amazing pizza), Potato Champion (amazing poutine), and Perierra Creperie (amazing Cinnamon Toast Crunch milkshake).

1204 SE Hawthorne Blvd
Portland, OR 97214

The Bonneville Hatchery

Apparently, the best time to visit is October through November. You'll see a bunch of salmon spawning then. I say go whenever.

70543 NE Herman Loop
Cascade Locks, OR 97014

Hood River, Oregon

It's just a nice town. There's a great Brewery there called Double Mountain. Take a significant other and make a day of it.

Keep Portland Weird

Even though Portland is pretty normal, you can get your very own bumper sticker at:

www.keepportlandweird.com

The Swifts

It's amazing. Bring a camera.

Chapman Elementary School
1445 NW 26th Ave
Portland, OR 97210

SUBSCRIBE TO EVERYTHING WE PUBLISH!

Do you love what Microcosm publishes?

Do you want us to publish more great stuff?

Would you like to receive each new title as it's published?

Subscribe as a BFF to our new titles and we'll mail them all to you as they are released!

$10-30/mo, pay what you can afford. Include your t-shirt size and your birthday for a possible surprise!

microcosmpublishing.com/bff

...AND HELP US GROW YOUR SMALL WORLD!

More love for Portland:

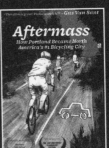

I don't know anything about this Portland. I'm sure it's nice.